broken hearts ...healing

young poets speak out on divorce

EDITED BY TOM WORTHEN, Ph.D.

Poet Tree Press
Logan, Utah

The poems are published in this book with the understanding that the poets and their parents or guardians have verified their originality.

Broken Hearts...Healing: Young Poets Speak Out on Divorce
©Copyright 2001, Poet Tree Press

Published by:
Poet Tree Press
90 North 100 East
Logan, Utah 84321
www.poettreepress.com
(435) 713-4414; fax: (435) 713-4422

ISBN 1-58876-150-9 (hardcover)   SAN: 253-6587
ISBN 1-58876-151-7 (softcover)

Printed in the United States of America

Suggested Cataloging in Publication Data

Worthen, Tom, 1959-
    Broken hearts..healing: young poets speak out on divorce.
        First Edition.
    1. Children of divorced parents — poetry.
    HQ 777.5.B76

Editor's Note
Call for Poems for Future Editions

The poems in this anthology were selected from poems entered in poetry contests sponsored by Creative Communication. Since 1993, Creative Communication has sponsored contests for poets in grades four to twelve. Poems of merit in these contests are published in the regional poetry anthology series *A Celebration of Young Poets*. The poems in *Broken Hearts...Healing* were selected from those published in past editions of *A Celebration of Young Poets*.

If you are interested in submitting a poem that will be considered for a future anthology published by Creative Communication or Poet Tree Press, then please follow the guidelines below to enter the contest. Each poem is first judged for admission into Creative Communication's *"A Celebration of Young Poets"* and then selections are considered for one of the books being created by Poet Tree Press for the *"Young Poets Speak Out"* series.

To have a poem considered for publication, please follow the guidelines listed below.

- **Only poets in grade 4-12 are considered**
- **21 Line maximum poem length**
- **Only one entry per student**
- **Poem must be the student's original work**
- **Any topic and any style are considered for publication**

> **Poems must be submitted with the student's**
> > **name (printed clearly)**
> > **grade and teacher's name**
> > **school name and address**
> > **home address**

> **Mail to: Poet Tree Press**
> > **P.O. Box 303**
> > **Smithfield, Utah 84335**

dedication

This book is dedicated to Kenne, Tim, and Kyrsti Worthen. It was your tears and mine that inspired the idea for this book.

I love you.

Dad

acknowledgements

This book was made possible by the poets who graciously allowed us to share their poems with others. They let us share their words so that others may heal.

A thank you goes to our illustrator, Kyle Hernandez. Kyle is a 3rd grade student at Summit Elementary in Smithfield, Utah who has received local and statewide recognition for his drawing. His unique perspective helped give a visual meaning to the chapters.

A special thanks goes to Elaine Litster. Elaine graciously spent many hours reading and re-reading each poem to help create the themes and chapters.

contents

foreword for parents ix
foreword for the youth xi
1 divorce changes everything 1
2 it happened to me 21
3 my heart is broken 33
4 whose fault is it? 47
5 i'm caught in the middle 57
6 i once had a family 75
7 you left me 85
8 you are missing my life 107
9 i don't love you 123
10 i miss you 133
11 i will always love you 147
12 i want my family back 163
13 my two homes 177
14 my evolving family tree 193
15 i'm still standing 211
16 lessons i've learned 227

foreword for parents

Divorce is a process. In the legal context it is a single event. To the individuals involved, divorce is a continuing cycle of love, hate, pain, fear and endless other emotions. The emotions felt depend on the parents and their relationship with each other; the children's relationship with their parents and step-parents; and the passing of time that can help healing occur or allow the bitterness to grow.

Having been divorced for over ten years, I still look back to the day I drove away from my children as the most painful day in my life. Since that time, I have suffered further pain by wanting and not having my children live with me. My pain comes, however, only from the pain that I see in my children. Divorce is most painful for the children.

After reading thousands of poetic testimonials from children of divorce, I found what often makes divorce most devastating is how the parents act and react toward each other and the children. Does the non-custodial parent make every attempt to be involved in the children's lives? Does the custodial parent support this involvement? One difference between a parent dying and leaving children behind and a parent absent due to divorce, is the feeling of abandonment. This is a feeling the custodial parent can enlarge or diminish. When step-parents are involved, are there four loving parents, or does competition for the child's love only pull the child into the awful middle? Some parents seem to feel that a child's love is like a glass of water. They feel there is only so much love to go around, and if too much love is given to the other parent, there will not be enough love left over. This attitude results in competition for the child's love. In contrast to the glass of water philosophy is that love is abundant, like water from a faucet. There is a never-ending supply. A parent doesn't need to put the other parent down in order to direct the child's love. Everyone can be loved.

Parents do not divorce children. When parents choose to be uninvolved in their child's life or when parents use children as a way to get back at the divorcing parent, the child suffers. The latter case reflects the *Medea* attitude, where a man or woman ends up hating his or her ex-spouse more than he or she loves the children. These parents often use the children as a tool to play out their role as a victim. When this occurs the divorce creates a series of painful victims with the children suffering the most.

As you read the poetic testimonials included in this book, I hope that they will speak to you. If you are contemplating a divorce I hope that this book will help you realize how that one decision ripples through many lives forever. If your children are experiencing the pain of a divorce, I hope these poems help you understand your children's emotions.

Many of the poems in this book describe the father as the parent that is not involved in the child's life. The selection of poems isn't meant to take sides, however, the poems that were reviewed for this book reflect society and the fact that most children of divorce live with their mothers.

The chapters are comprised of the themes that emerged from the poems. Each chapter reinforces the research on the stages that individuals go through after a divorce. Whereas several of the poems could have been placed in different chapters, the placement that was chosen for each poem reflects the overall concept for the book and the subjective nature of editing a book of poetry.

Knowing that the pain, frustration and love expressed in each poem are real, a strong emotional reaction is created. These are children much like yours and mine; children who are reaching out through their poetry to find an audience who will listen. Thank you for lending an ear.

Tom Worthen, Ph.D.
June 2001

foreword for the youth

In the words of my children, "Divorce sucks." Having your parents end their marriage changes your whole world. But you are not alone.

The idea to create this book came from my three children when they felt they were the only kids at their school whose parents were divorced. In reality, several of their teachers and many of their classmates came from divorced families. However, they felt alone in their frustrations. Knowing that other kids across the country share your feelings can let you know you are not alone, and your world doesn't end with the ending of a marriage. Hopefully, you will come to the conclusion that you are still loved even though your world has painfully changed.

The authors of the poems in this book are children age nine to eighteen who have experienced many of the emotions you have. They have been afraid, lonely, angry and loved. You may not relate to every poem in this book. However, I hope that you can find comfort by reading the poems of other children who share many of your feelings.

Tom Worthen, Ph.D.
June 2001

divorce changes everything

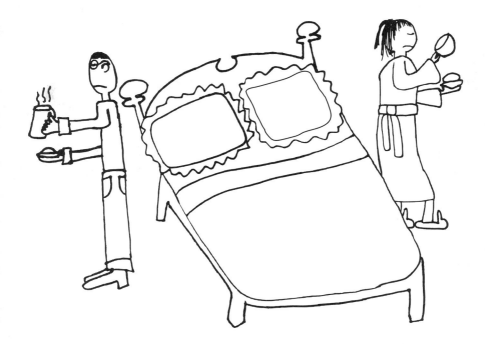

Disappearance

Divorce to me is
pain and agony,
but mostly sadness.

Divorce is
crying and
separation
and people lost
from view.

Divorce to me is
like being on a
drug until
reality comes
to hurt and
haunt you
forever.

Divorce is knowing
life will go on,
but without being
the same ever again.

Chloe
Texas
Age 11

Broken Hearts

Divorces aren't good
Kids don't like them
There are broken hearts
That sometimes don't heal
Little ones cry
It's a lot of money to waste
It's very painful
And changes your life forever
And it is very, very sad
People cry and children cry
I don't like divorces at all
It's like painting a picture
The paint never comes off
Like a divorce affects your life

Mikal
Michigan
Age 9

Divorce

Divorce is like a scare,
that will never go away inside.
Divorce is like a scrape,
that makes you want to cry.

Divorce is like a burn,
that will hurt for so long.
Divorce is no good,
Divorce is so wrong.

Why do people do it?
I guess I'll never know.
If they loved each other from the start,
then why do they let each other go?

Dawn
Ohio
Age 13

I Wish

I wish I could change the past.
To go back into time.
To when my parents' marriage started having problems.
I wish I could work on the problems
So my parents would still be together
And I could have a father again.
I don't know my father.

> Is he rich?
> Is he poor?
> Do I have any siblings?
> Does he even care?

I wish I could make the pain go away
But to do that would be to do the impossible.
If I could change the past my life would be totally different.

> Different friends
> Different house
> Different neighborhood
> Different me!

Danielle
Pennsylvania
Age 13

I Am Different

I would be different, they would be different, everything would be different.
We were all hurt, with our salty tears flooding the earth
I would be different, they would be different, everything would be different.
The yelling was over, at least in person, but there were still the telephone wars
When all I would hear was "No Allen!", "Yes, Susan!"
When they were arguing about me or arguing about them
I would be different, they would be different, everything would be different.
The boxes stacked up all over, seeing my toys gone, packed away in plain
        brown boxes
I didn't know who packed those boxes, but I knew it took courage and a stiff
        upper lip
I would be different, they would be different, everything would be different.
Would it ever end? Of course it would, but when?
When could I feel free, feel free of all the conflicts around me
The fighting was like a knife, cutting through my heart, breaking everything I knew
I would be different, they would be different, everything would be different.
I needed someone to talk to but no one was in sight
Everyone has their own problems, they don't have to hear mine
I would be different, they would be different, everything would be different.
The contradictions created a world around me filled with confusion and hurt
        feelings
One parent would say yes, the other would say no
I am different, they are different, everything is different.

Jennifer
New York
Age 12

Love to Hate

How can two people
love each other so much,
then become enemies
and hate each other and such?

I just don't understand
all the hate that they hold.
When I watch them fight
their feelings seem so old.

Can't they remember
all the love that they shared?
And they would try harder to get along,
that is, if they even cared!

Consumed in their petty arguments
they forget the most important things.
Their children's hearts are broken
but I guess that's the consequence fighting brings.

But they are too immature
to work things out,
and they will never understand
what their fighting was all about.

Shelly
California
Age 15

8

Ten

I thought my life was a total disaster.
My parents were fighting day and night.
They split up. I was ten.

I had two sisters that needed me,
so I couldn't cry when my parents fought.
One day they just kept getting louder. I was ten.

One day I came home. My dad was not there.
I ran into my room and
slammed the door. I was ten.

Maybe it was better for them.
Maybe it wasn't. But I still knew
I loved them both. I was ten.

I loved you both so very much,
but you did not love each other.
When I was ten.

Christine
Ohio
Age 12

They Should Not Have

They shouldn't have done it now.
They should never do it.
They are meant for each other.
I thought they would be together forever.
Now is not a good time.
Didn't the vows mean more to them?

My whole world is being turned up-side-down.
At the very least, wait till I move out of the house.
Did I do something wrong?
I feel so alone as if no one understands.

A divorce was not the answer for them.
It is as if they were sweeping the dirt under the rug.
Instead of dealing with their problems,
they are taking the easy way out.

Jason
Oregon
Age 14

Pain and Tears

Divorce is a thing that happens everyday,
People breaking marriages with nothing more to say.
Pain and tears is what divorce should be called,
Because ever since the announcement all I've done is bawled.

It is so unfair,
The way parents can do things without a single care.
And break a child's heart,
Because they decide to part.
What are we supposed to do?
The pain to me is so brand new.

"Why me?"
Is what I ask from He.
But His reply, I've yet to receive.

I just can't understand,
How you can give up on that wedding band,
And figure that the marriage is no more
And step outside and slam the door.

And separating without a try,
And in this problem, you have failed to pry.

Heather
Ohio
Age 13

When Is It Over?

Is it over when the anniversary flowers are left in the trash by the door?
Or is it the solitude and silent ending of a life?
Two lives torn apart – and by what?
Is it the clanging of change and the crackling of crisp bills?
Or is it something deep within us that says "I give up; it's time to let go?"
Or is it the children's faces, the tears in our pillows at night?
The happy days shattered by yelling nights

And why?

The Love?
But we all know things will change.
The Children?
Oh in time all wounds will heal.
Or will they?
The Money?
But what about fun?
The Money?
But what about pride?
The Money?
But does it matter?
But dad is gone–
and mom is crying–

Elissa
California
Age 13

Divorce

He gets this,
You get that.
What do I get?
Well, let me tell you.

Dad gets the car,
You get the house,
I get the "It's not your fault" speech.

Dad gets the big screen TV,
You get the stereo system,
I get a little brother who doesn't understand.

Dad gets the lawn furniture,
You get the garden gnomes,
I get the heartache.

Dad gets the microwave,
You get the couch,
I get the tears.

Dad gets the summer house,
You get the crystal chandelier,
I get the sleepless nights.

You both get what you want,
Why can't I get what I want?

Melissa
New York
Age 16

A Look to a Brighter Sky

Divorce is something I sometimes wish weren't true,
for it turns all skies a dark blue.

It doesn't matter if you win or lose,
the final decision always leaves a nasty bruise.

Some think it is no big deal,
but to kids it's a never ending deal.

Trust me -- it will go straight to your heart.
You're scared to have to see them apart.

It sometimes feels like arguments will never end,
and yet all you can do is try to contend.

Hopefully someone might lead you to an open road,
to sit with and listen to your feelings unfold.

You may think that it is not the best thing to do,
but when you let your feelings hide, you create a miserable you.

Sometimes you think the feelings of hurt you can't express,
but then you find to tell will create less mess.

Give yourself a chance -- it will do your body good.

Don't forget to keep your head high
and always look for the brighter sky.

Just remember, it's divorce; it's not your fault,
and never bring yourself to a complete halt.

Melissa
New Jersey
Age 14

Changes

Sometimes change can be good,
Or terrible.
When I was little,
Things changed all the time,
We moved a lot.
My dad was home but was soon gone.
My brother was born,
And the house turned upside down.
We left my dad and moved in with my grandma,
Then moved to a house of our own.
After my parents divorced we came to Colorado,
Then tremendous changes were made.
I went to a big school,
And had a lot of nasty words said about me.
I was called names,
And was always burnt on the inside.
From the burns, I still have scar tissue,
That gets opened every once in a while.
This is what happens,
When your world changes,
For the worst.

Amanda
Colorado
Age 15

Divorce

Divorce can slaughter you,
Screaming for hours,
Feeling in the center,
Feeling terrible,
Blaming inside,
Running to your room,
Slam, you slam your door,
Tears fall like rain,
Gazing at them as they hit the carpet,
Wondering will it ever end,
You hear the word divorce,
It kills you,
You never thought it could turn out so bad,
Divorce is terrible.

Jonathan
New Mexico
Age 11

Why Do I Feel So Bad?

Mommy and Daddy fight every night,
So why do I feel so bad?
They argue over little things,
But the little things turn into big problems.
Being the middle child, I wonder more
Why people fight or just why do my parents fight?
Is it because they love us more than each other,
Or because they are going through changes.
But being divorced isn't the best thing,
So why do I feel so bad?

Tanisha
New York
Age 11

When One Walks Away

Many people say
That kids could never know
What it means
When their parents get divorced
But that is all just a lie
Kids know what it means
When one parent says good-bye
They know what it means
When one walks away
And the other one holds you
And says it will be okay
When one walks away
And never comes back.

Nicole
Michigan
Age 15

Mommy and Daddy

Thank you for all that you have given.
The nails in my heart that you have driven.
What have I done? What can I do?
To bring back the family that I once knew.
Now there is nothing, love is no more.
Fantasies of happiness are now a bore.
I am older now and numb to the pain.
But in my memories is still a stain.
Bad things done, no remorse.
All this pain because of divorce.

Leo
Michigan
Age 17

it happened
to me

I Remember When

I remember when I learned my parents got divorced,
My mom sat me down
and tried to explain why.
I just sat there and stared.
She said,
"Your dad and I must go
our separate ways."
I didn't know what
That meant,
So I just shook my head.

Cameron
New Mexico
Age 14

My Questions

As if I didn't notice all the recent fights
I knew what was coming and I was confused
My knees tucked under my chin
Swaying to the beat of anticipation
I knew what was coming
They acted as if I hadn't known
They hadn't lived in the same room for months
How are we a family
If we don't live in the same house
How are you going to say you love me
If I only see you once a week
"We are getting divorced." My mom's words rang in my ear
As my sister ran to her room crying
I buried my face in my knees
Trying to choke the tears inside
Tears leaked down my face
Me, unaware of the warm streams of water that treaded down my cheeks
Unlike most, I didn't blame myself
It was their fault, I knew it was
And the final question:
Why did you have to do this to me?

Lia
New Mexico
Age 14

These Words

For the longest time I knew something was not right.
I was constantly wondering until that day
They sat me down in the kitchen.
They didn't say anything, but I started to cry.
Then those words came out.
The same words that haunt me every night.
I closed my eyes but they didn't go away.
Every night I cried myself to sleep.
I wished I was dreaming.
I wished it wasn't real.
I've kept these feelings inside of me for a long time,
Until they've burned a hole in my gut.
I can't think straight,
I can't concentrate.
All I can think of are these words.
The words that make me hurt so much.
They said it would be okay.
But will it?
I may never know.

Jackie
New York
Age 11

Time After Time

I sit up in my bed.
I hear a lot of noise.
I see my parents arguing
Like two arch rival boys.

I try to stop their fighting,
But they just ignore me.
Instead of treating me like a teenager,
They treat me like a little bee.

I lie down on my bed
Trying to go to sleep.
I listen to the door slam,
Then I do not hear a single peep.

My parents are still mad,
But still I wonder why?
They tell me what they're going to do
And then I start to cry.

Travis
Virginia
Age 13

Twelve

Up in Youngstown a day in May
I was sitting by my sister,
We were reading magazines.
We sat for hours and hours.
It was hard, I was twelve.

I saw lawyers, secretaries, and cops
All doing their jobs.
There was a tour group,
I sat there with my sister.
I was twelve.

I thought to myself,
"What would it be like?
What would I do?
Why did this have to happen?"
I was twelve.

I was sitting, then my parents came out.
They told me it was almost over.
They came out a half hour later
and my parents were divorced.

I was riding home, depressed,
I was twelve.

Brad
Ohio
Age 12

Divorce

Since my mother said those words many years have passed by
They have haunted my ears forever and put a few tears in my eye
I was just a little child then and it could not seem so true
And I finally understood the phrase, "It could happen to you"
I always thought it would be a word that seemed so lifeless and fake
But instead had put a hole in me that no shovel could ever make
And through my confusion and tears, I finally understood
My mom was taking us away and leaving my dad for good
My brother was just a toddler then and he did not know why
His dad was never around but yet he never seemed to cry
And though my mom's voice was very hard and coarse
I could hear the words perfectly,
They were getting a divorce.

Chelsea
Maine
Age 13

Daddy's Little Girl

From the other side of the world he brought me a "kimono."
It was beautiful; he had one too.
In them, we pose, he kneeling and I leaning.
He holds me as if I were glass:
A China doll not to be shattered.
His chin to the crown of my head,
I am a princess.

Around us are the pieces of my parents' marriage.
The Sony television that has lasted till this day,
The solid, wooden bookcases that still stand,
And books on tables, everywhere.

Three years later in the same room
my parents sat, faces sober and drawn,
on opposite ends of the room.
Shelves, television, and books between them,
A great, yawning distance.

My mother took the books,
My father stole the bookshelves.
Mother bargained for the television,
Father fought for the table.

And Mother won the children.

Erin
Connecticut
Age 17

Divorce

It's that word that everyone dreads,
To even think about it in their heads.
It's that word that makes you sad,
It just makes everyone feel bad.
What would you do if your parents came home one day,
And just said, "Let's get a divorce right away."
It's not that easy for me,
It was like getting stung by one hundred bees.
Today in front of me it was said.
I wanted to lay down forever in my bed,
I just wanted to cry,
I wanted to curl up and die.
You see you are not alone.
Maybe, just maybe things will get better at home.

Kristin
Wisconsin
Age 11

my heart
is broken

The Child

The parents fought and fussed.
The child watched in disgust.
The parents so wrapped up in themselves,
Never thought of the child's health.
The father who moved away,
Still doesn't care to this day.
The parents went on with their lives,
The child grew with tears in her eyes.
Eleven years later and they don't care,
That the child feels like they're never there.
The parents never knew,
That the child was broken in two.

Nikki
Alabama
Age 13

It Did Affect Me

The day you told me,
The world stopped spinning.
And my little five-year-old life came to a screeching halt,
I don't understand.
I was so young, you thought I wouldn't remember,
But I do.
I was so young, you thought it wouldn't affect me,
But it did.
It seemed like just yesterday,
We were a family,
Now it seems to be falling apart.
My heart was ripped in two,
And I had all these mixed feelings.
Frustration, anger, sadness, misery, all wrapped up in one heart.
Sometimes, I feel like crying for no reason,
And I ask God why He did it,
But I know He didn't do it to hurt me.
I'm still healing, so let's take things slow,
Even though I was young, you see,
It did affect me.

Meghan
California
Age 13

Where Does the Love Go?

I should know.
My parents are divorced.
It's a hatred thing.
When my parents got divorced,
My heart felt like a stone.
It shatters the heart
Like a window hit by a ball.

They don't love each other anymore.
How can you run out of love?
It's the "devil's curse!"
Why should there be such a thing as divorce?
It sounds like a dying bird.
The love is just dead.
There is no more love.

Julia
Michigan
Age 11

Twelve

In my home there was a disaster.
I came home to find out that my mother did not love my father anymore.
I was Twelve.

When I saw his eyes start to water I burst into tears.
It felt like a ton of bricks falling on my head.
I was Twelve.

I don't think my mother knew how much she was hurting my father.
They tried to work it out but it just didn't happen.
I knew I had to be strong for my brothers and sisters.
I was only Twelve.

Eric
Ohio
Age 14

I Am

I am a worried kid whose parents are divorced
I constantly wonder if what I'm doing is best for me
I hear the tortured cries from within my own body and soul
I see that I'm a nuclear explosion of misery and sorrow
I want for all of the pain to end now
I am a worried kid whose parents are divorced.

I pretend that everything is normal and it usually is
I feel divorce's pressure on my already heavy shoulders
I touch the burning flame of sadness in my heart, and cringe
I worry about my own fading health that I've neglected
I cry when I think about my recent life
I am a worried kid whose parents are divorced.

I understand that my life will never be the same
I say things that betray myself and my heart
I dream that things will be better soon
I try to keep my real emotions from showing, for they hurt
I hope that the constant pain of a divorce will go away soon
I am a worried kid whose parents are divorced.

Andrew
Louisiana
Age 12

Dream in My Pocket

I have a dream in my pocket,
I have my life in the other,
I just can't decide between one or the other.
I have my mom in my pocket,
I have my dad in the other,
Even though they don't seem to get along with each other, they still stay together.
I have a divorce paper in my pocket,
I have my parents in the other,
If they don't start getting along they might leave each other.
I have a knife in my pocket,
I have my life in the other,
Who knows what will happen if things don't start getting better?
I have a dream in my pocket that will be there forever.

Tricia
Ohio
Age 15

The Structure of Family

It feels like a stabbing knife through your heart
You're sad and cry day and night
Parents never wanting to talk to each other
Always mad and frustrated
Feeling every word people say is an insult toward you
Your heart breaking into small shattered pieces all over the place
Wanting to go away and scream out loud
All your feelings inside of your mind
Family problems starting to get bigger and bigger every minute of the day
Wanting not to talk to anyone
Just to be alone
Wishing every second of your life
Your parents to get back together once more
Forever your insides will feel like gushing and bursting

Daisy
New Mexico
Age 11

Divorce

Divorce is like a wild horse walking through your heart
It destroys your feelings and separates you from your loved ones for a long time
It hurts your heart
You start to cry
You wish you were dead
You feel like running away from everything around you
You wish they were together forever
You wish you were dead
You want to kill yourself
You wish you were somebody else
You hate it when you see them fighting over something so stupid
You wish they would just forget everything that wasn't true
You hate it when they don't listen to you
You miss their good night kisses

Javier
New Mexico
Age 12

Betrayal

Betrayal is black like a shut coffin
On a pitch dark night
And also like wet dirt.
It creeps through my soul.
It reminds me of the time
My parents got divorced.
It makes me feel lonely
Like a tree blowing in the wind
On a cold fall night.
It makes me want to
DIE!

Nick
Iowa
Age 13

Divorce

The breaking of a window,
The shattering of a door,
There are some sounds in your mind,
But there are many more.
Never in my life, I would have expected
Something so awful, so resented.
Hoping it would leave,
Like a trick from your sleeve.
Unfortunately it did not
Leaving me with nothing but a heart full taut
Dear God, help me as I struggle,
Help me not to fall or stumble
Upon the many rocks in life.

Jennifer
North Carolina
Age 10

44

whose fault is it?

Whose Fault?

A child waits atop the stairs
Saying nothing, he only stares.

Listening to his parents fight,
Hear them holler throughout the night.

Who's at fault
Me or the adult?

Moving here, moving there,
I try to act like I just don't care.

Soon follows a divorce,
And my parents have no remorse.

I still ponder about that question
The one that I dare not mention.

Brandon
Ohio
Age 14

It Killed My Self Esteem

Before when I was perfect
you were always around
but now that I am not
you can never be found
What did I do
to make you desert me
let me know how to fix it
please, why won't you tell me
I must have been bad
to deserve all this pain
even when we are together
it all seems in vain
What did I do
to fall from your heart
what did I do
to tear this family apart
please tell me, what have I done
I guess I am just a terrible son
all I can say is that I am sorry
and I beg of you
please do not hate me

Chaz
California
Age 16

That Word, Divorce

I had a broken heart,
My family was apart.
It was all my fault,
And my tears were bitter salt.

I felt like the only one,
They did what had to be done.
I was a sad puppy with no home,
My father had just moved out on his own.

I couldn't eat, I couldn't sleep,
My father gave me a present to keep.
Miserable and sad,
I wasn't too glad.

My throat throbbing with pain,
My life was never the same.
I felt pounded like an ant becoming flat,
My family was as unlucky as the color black.

I bluster and blame,
But it isn't the same.
I say it was me,
But how can that be?

Tony
New Jersey
Age 11

My Father

My father is never there.
He acts as though he doesn't care.
He is never there to play,
and he never has anything to say.
It's been so long since he's called
to say "Hi" "How are you?" and never
"I love you."
I used to wonder what I did
but now I know it wasn't me.
It's him.

Laura
Ohio
Age 13

Divorce

You feel like your world is split in half
By your own parents' wrath.

It makes you cry
And ask yourself why?

Was it the loss of trust?
Or the loss of lust?

Was it because they could not stand each other?
Or was there a different lover?

You feel empty, and want the pain to go away
So you can smile, and be gay.

But, you have to take life with a grain of salt
And not blame yourself for the fault.

Traci
Arizona
Age 14

Why Do the Kids Pay?

Sometimes I cry,
But I pretend I don't know why.

But I do,
It's because I want to know you.

I've seen pictures and heard both sides,
When I tell my mom I want to see you, she only sighs.

I don't know who to believe.
And anyway, what would that achieve?

It really doesn't matter,
It only makes me sadder.

I wish you were here, I wish you would come.
You should make up all the years you missed, at least some.

Is it my fault? Did I do something wrong?
'Cause I don't see what I did to ruin a father-daughter bond.

I try to hold back and fight the pain,
But how is a 12-year-old supposed to do that and stay sane?

I hope to see you again some day
So you can answer my question: in divorce, why do the kids pay?

Stephanie
Nevada
Age 12

i'm caught
in the middle

Which Limb Am I?

I have two sets of parents.
I'm lucky, you say.
Just try being in my shoes
Every other Friday.

"I Love You!"
"I Love You more!!"
Oh somebody, please somebody
Get me out of this tug-of-war.

The lawyers and judges,
They all play a part
In creating a torn, shattered and broken heart.

I know I'm not alone,
There are lots of kids like me
With a horribly complicated family tree.

Colleen
Pennsylvania
Age 11

Loss

They were yelling at each other, I could hear them clearly,
not again, this began a month ago, and they couldn't stop.
I told them to stop, but my mom told me to go play with my friends.
I hate it when they fight, but what do they care?
They are getting divorced anyway, so they will be arguing for a long time.
The next day, my mom took me and showed me her new apartment
which was a piece of junk until we took a few hours cleaning it.
My dad said that I would see him every Wednesday, Saturday, and Sunday.
Then my mom went to court to fight for her full possession of me,
but she lost, and now, she and my father always fight.
I haven't been able to sit close to either of them
and not hear about how wrong they say each other is about something.
I will never hear their good sides of each other, not that I ever have.

Cyrus
California
Age 12

Why Me?

I'm sitting here alone up in my room
Thinking about everything our family has been through.
I just think back in time, and it gives me the chills
Watching our family go downhill.
First it just starts out with arguments,
Then divorce and at that time I didn't even want to
Know what would happen next.
Hearing two different stories from each side of the family
Having no clue who to believe
You'd wish this was all a dream
Then you stop and wonder,
Why Me?

Victoria
Ohio
Age 13

Separated

Why can't some couples stay together?
Why can't they just love each other forever?
Who even started things like that?
They say their wedding vows,
Then one of them's gone, like the drop of a hat.
Why can't they just hug and make up with each other?
That's what I'm supposed to do with my brother!
You feel like a pullstring being pulled in either direction,
Both of them wanting your love and affection.
But you have to love both, you can't love just one.
You just want them back together. This is no fun.
You're all confused and shaken up inside.
Especially when you feel that one of them has lied.
Your whole life is filled with sadness and remorse.
And that's what happens when your parents get a divorce.

Whitney
New York
Age 13

In the Middle

I love my mother
Because she is like no other.
I love my father
Because his love goes much farther.

I love my mother for grace.
(Now that's something that cannot be replaced!)
I love my father for his pride,
Which he cannot put aside.

I love my mother because she is strong
And is almost never wrong.
I love my father because he is always himself
And will not change for anyone else.

My parents are all these things and more
And I am the one they both adore.
But because they do not love each other anymore,
I am standing between two doors.

And I'm in the middle of the two people I love the most,
But I want to disappear like a ghost
Back to the world
When I was *their* little girl.

Carla
South Carolina
Age 14

Parents

My mom doesn't get along with my dad
And this makes me very sad
For I do get along with my dad
And this makes my mother mad
I want to go live with my dad
But my mother says that's bad
But I think that it would be good
And I think that I should

But life here isn't so bad
And leaving would make my mother sad
So here I am torn between the two
And still I don't know what to do.

Bryan
California
Age 12

The Big Decision

When the time comes I will have to make
A decision.
My future's at stake.

When the time comes I will not know
What to do.
So I wish it were up to you.

I can choose my mom or dad.
But I'll leave one behind
And feel terribly sad.

I've been with her all my life.
My mom, I know,
Has helped me grow.

I love Dad so because he's so nice.
He keeps me safe
With his good advice.

I'm concerned
I'll make a mistake
With this decision I have to make.

Ted
Michigan
Age 12

Yelling and Screaming, What's Next?

Every night I used to sit at home in my room listening to my mom and dad fight,
It's always about bills,
Who made the bed that morning,
How much money you spent,
Why aren't you ever home any more,
Things from the top to the bottom of the list,
My sister would come into my room at night so she wouldn't have to be alone
     at night,
We snuggle up and wish, hope, and pray that they will stop fighting,
Now the time has come,
Do I go with mom or dad?
I want to stay with both,
So the judge will compromise,
Now I have two homes,
Two rooms,
I just look at the ups of the problem,
And ignore the downs,
Will the fighting ever stop?

Michaela
Wyoming
Age 12

One or the Other

Left to choose between one or the other
Not willing to do it but so close to her mother

Picking and choosing what will the other think
Will her choice make the other parent's heart want to sink

Put in the middle is not the place she wants to be
Will the other understand and will they see

She's cried and cried till her eyes can cry no more
Making her want to escape the pain and just run out the door

Telling herself over and over again she didn't cause this mess
It's not her fault and hoping the other won't think of her any less

How could this whole mess break an innocent child's heart
When will the pieces be put back together after being torn apart

Melissa
New Hampshire
Age 17

Spl/it

It's like a knife
Cutting a family in two
One half lives here, breathing a sigh of relief.
The other is left gasping for air.
It's hard to get through
Without thinking of how it used to be.
The puzzle that was once linked together
Is now pieces of scattered memories.

I want to make new memories
And put the pieces back together.
I'm trying but it's hard for me to do.
There is a part of me that wants
To be in both places at the same time,
Back with my father,
Yet never leaving my mother.
I am cast aside like a puzzle piece
That doesn't fit in, yet.
The memories are just pieces.
They live at my father's house,
Locked up in a box of old toys.

Alexandra
Connecticut
Age 13

Tough Decision

I have a very big decision to make.
Too bad it's not as easy as baking a cake.
No matter what choice I choose
I know there is something I'm going to lose.
My step-dad wants me to change my last name.
But if I do I know I won't be the same.
I know that if I say I don't want to
Then he probably won't treat me like he used to.
I love my step-dad just as any girl would.
And I would change it if I could.
But I know my heart just wouldn't feel right.
Not having anything to remember my real father just gives me a fright.
Even though I don't see my real dad.
I love him just like I always had.
I want to tell my step-dad, "I love you,
Don't be mad, but unfortunately my answer is I don't want to."

Anna Marie
Texas
Age 13

Divorce

Swearing,
      Screaming,
           Fighting
Like a vicious lion tormenting its prey;
A black hole you will never escape.
An arrow piercing the heart as
Two angels descend into the fiery pits of hell,
Changing so many lives forever—
With me.
      Watching it all.

Jolynn
Wisconsin
Age 13

War

My family is at war!!!
   Always fighting as if
   there is NO END!!!
They plan their attacks
   while I am at the other
   parent's house!!!
Then they ATTACK!!!!!!
They attack on the phone
   or at dad's driveway!!!

Meagan
Michigan
Age 12

Tug of War

Nobody has the life I have,
I can't imagine if the whole world did.

My parents don't even talk,
They get us to ask who wants us and when.
It is like me and my two sisters are in the middle of everything.

So I hope you don't have the life I have,
And if you do I'm sorry.

Beth
Pennsylvania
Age 11

i once had a family

Family

I once had a family who would love one another.
I once had a family who cared a lot.
I once had a family who stuck together.
I once had a family who did things together.
I once had a family who ate every meal together.
I once had a family with good compliments for everyone.
I once had a family who tried their best to stick together.
I once had a family who tried not to fight.
I once had a family who couldn't try any more.
I once had a family that was ready to break up.
I once had a family who couldn't stand it any more.
I once had a family and now I don't have one.

Betsy
Michigan
Age 11

Four Broken Hearts

What happened?
  What happened?

  They fought
        and
          fought
  yelled
        and
          cried
        and
  got further
        and
  further
          apart
  but most of
          all
  there
          were
  four
          broken
  hearts

What happened?
  What happened?

                    Jeremy
                  New Jersey
                   Age 10

I Remember

I remember the yelling and the screaming,
The arguing and the fighting,
The silence and the whispering,
I remember that night.

I remember the papers, the separation.
I remember how it ate me up inside,
With nothing to let out
Not even a tear drop to cry.
The love that used to flow in the air we breathed,
The times that we used to play around,
When we laughed and had nothing else better to do.

I remember we made a great team,
And how we fell apart, piece by piece.
I remember how I thought it was all my fault
And that this couldn't be happening.

I remember where we went,
I remember I missed my family.

I remember I loved them.

Trisha
New Hampshire
Age 13

Dead Love

I listened quietly at the bedroom door.
As they yelled vicious things at each other.
I went to sleep that night around four.
My dad had told my mom he loved another.

My doleful heart was breaking slowly.
My mom and dad were getting a divorce.
He told her so hatefully and coldly.
When he told her, she slapped him with force.

Will her soft cries and wet tears fall forever?
Though I hug her and tell her it'll be okay.
She looks up at my face and whispers never.
When I turn to leave she asks me to stay.

My parents will never be good friends.
I guess all my dreams must come to an end.

Jeanne
Louisiana
Age 16

Broken Promises

How do they ever manage to survive,
I ask myself confused.
Living out endless battles between good and evil,
For love is something they most certainly strive.
At one time they thought their love would thrive.

How could they put me in a situation I can't escape?
Why did they do this to me?
I'm in the middle of a never-ending quarrel.
Mommy's little angel, and Daddy's little girl,
It's difficult to believe, but it's exactly what I see.

Every day I literally cry myself to sleep,
Wishing it was all a horrible nightmare.
This family together is what I wish I could keep,
But, it's too late now, they shattered their special bond.
One that should have never been broken.

Meghan
Michigan
Age 13

Why?

My parents have been together,
For over fifteen years.
They've gone through it all,
Through the joys and the tears.

I sit here all alone,
Crying on my bed.
With the words they told me,
Repeating in my head.

They said they were breaking up,
And that I wasn't to blame.
And even though they were apart,
It would still stay the same.

Sometimes I wish they hadn't split up,
So they'd both be here with me.
Even though I know,
We'll never be a happy family.

Robert
Louisiana
Age 13

you left me

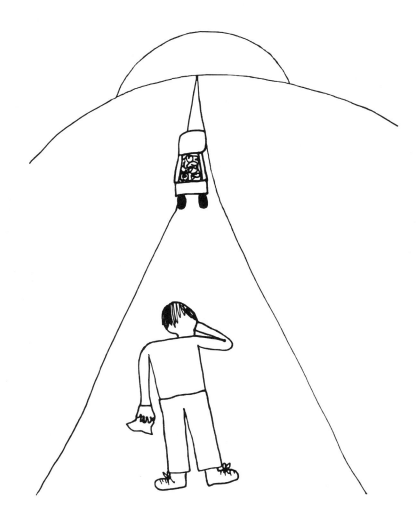

Why Did He Go?

It all happened so fast
I don't remember everything.
    My father left the house
And I didn't see him
    very often
Why did he go?
    Why did he go?
My father
    used to
play
    with
me.
    Now
only 36 times a year I get
    to see
    him.
I wish
    I could
see him
    more
Why did he go?
    Why did he go?

Christopher
New Jersey
Age 10

Memories

Mom told me
about him.
When I was born
he ran down the hallway
in the hospital.
He rocked me to sleep
every night.
She told me
how he carried me
everywhere.
How he bought me
everything I wanted.

When I turned one he said,
"Everything will be all right."
Then I turned two.
He was gone.
I could not find him
anywhere.
That's the only thing
I remember
of him.

Takieta
Alabama
Age 11

How Could You?

How could you do this to me?
Leave me, four years old
Standing there, on a cold November day
With only a kiss on the cheek, and a hug.
Leave me alone for five years
With no one, except mom
How could you leave me with no father?
Disappear from my life,
Just leave me
Like I was a penny that you dropped
Never to be picked up,
Because I was worth nothing to you!
Never turning around
To see what would happen
To my future and mom's.
And then someone comes along,
A loving step-father,
No, not the same.
No more taking walks, and no more piggy-back rides.
That's all I remember
How could you??

Keisha
Pennsylvania
Age 13

A Summer of Change

I remember
When my Dad called from his cell phone
He said he wanted a divorce.
He went away to think about himself
But that was a lie.
He went to cheat and screwed things up forever
For my Mom and me.
He drove down the steep driveway
To the new house that was supposed to hold great promise.
Mom and I, a mix of emotion,
Scared, crying, bewildered.
He said he wanted a divorce–a new chance at an exciting life.
I think about the day my Dad asked for a divorce.
And I quiver with fear and sadness.
I see my Dad differently today. Not as a Dad who was there for me,
But a weak, self-centered person who has no dignity.
I remember being in counseling class,
Breaking down barriers,
Seeking a better relationship with my Dad,
But the hole in my chest will never mend.

Joshua
New Jersey
Age 12

He Left Without Saying "Good-bye"

I regret that I just stood there.
Now I wish that I had said something.
My dad packed up and moved right out.
Maybe if I had never talked back,
My life would still be the same.
I wish sometimes he'd be there
To watch me grow up and change.
Many things go on in my head,
Like I still wish he'd change his mind,
And return to his old life with us.
I wonder if he sits at night
Wishing to turn back time
Or if he even wants to notice
What he's missed through the years.
And all the things that have changed in my life.
But as I'm getting older
I realize he's not coming.
Without him my life is like a donut;
There will always be a part of it somewhere else.

Shari
Missouri
Age 16

A Lying Love

The last time that I saw him,
Was seven months ago.
I saw him on my birthday,
And the other months went slow.

No calls, letters or e-mail,
Can fix this pain I have.
I've called him once or twice before,
But I always end up mad.

Sometimes I think I miss him,
From having no other dad.
From all the pain he's put me through,
I'd rather just be sad.

I guess he doesn't need us,
Since he's got his brand new life.
A brand new house and two little kids,
And a very special wife.

He always knew how to make me laugh,
But now he makes me cry,
Leaving me so long ago
His love seemed like a lie.

Sarah
Ohio
Age 13

The Man

There was a man
That I once knew,
He left his home
And his family too.

He met a girl
Which he lives with now,
But I don't care
He's on his own for awhile.

This man I knew
He is my dad,
I never see him
But I'm not mad.

He used to be great
And was a good guy,
Now he acts like he's eight
And I can't look him in the eye.

Jon
West Virginia
Age 13

Daddy's Girl

From the moment I was born, from my first little curl
I was always told that I was a daddy's girl.
I look like my dad a lot of people say
But now they do not say that, because he moved away.
Away someplace, I don't know; he said he couldn't stay
He simply packed his leather bag, moved and went away.
He never, ever calls and I don't see him a lot
And now for the rest of my life, my soul's tied in a knot.
You have to hold thoughts up inside of you, hoping that today
Would be the day he calls, so you sit and pray.
You go to special therapy, because you can't think straight
Without seeing your dad, your buddy and soul mate.
He lives somewhere else, just not with me
Somewhere happier than before, so I guess his life is free.
As free as a bird that flies way up high
As free as a rainbow shining in the sky.
He's where he wants to be and he couldn't be more happy.
To screw up my life and then take off without me.
I love my mom a lot, but I'm just really sad
That I'm a little daddy's girl
Just without a dad.

Megan
Pennsylvania
Age 14

A Girl Without

A girl without her father is incomplete
She doesn't know how to rough house,
Or to sing rock.
She doesn't know what a bear hug is,
Or a playful punch.
She doesn't know about the loving bunkbed,
Or the feeling of a belly pillow.
She doesn't know what "Daddy's Girl" means,
Or the nickname he gives to her.
She cannot hear his cheers in the crowd,
Or the sound of, "That's my girl."
She cannot feel his strong arms squeezing her tight,
Or the sound of his soft voice tucking her in at night.
She cannot say, "My dad does this,"
Or, "My dad does that."
She cannot enjoy cruising in the car,
Or playing outdoors.
She can't lean on his shoulder,
Or cry in his arms.
But most of all, she can't say, "I love you Dad"
And him reply, "I love you too."

Megan
Virginia
Age 13

Good Intentions

He doesn't come around any more
His time with us is past,
As if we had been wiped off the globe by some atomic blast.

Sometimes I try to look inside him,
But much to my dismay,
The only thing I find are empty promises made to pass some time away.

Sometimes I look upon him,
As if through a looking glass,
And all I see is a time before when summers were a thousand laughs
And love between a father and daughter meant so much more.

Germaine
Pennsylvania
Age 17

A Note Of Grief To My "Father" . . .

Why at the time I needed you most you decided to leave me
Do you think it did not hurt when you left
Do you think because I have a mother that I don't need you
Well you think wrong because Father I love you,
I know I may not show it all the time—But I do
Just the other day when I realized that you had left
without calling or even leaving a letter
it hurt
I understand that you have other responsibilities now,
because you have a wife and another child,
But what about me, *I am also your child!*
For once Father I would like for you to think about
me and how I feel
Did it ever occur to you that I may have a question
or a problem that I would like for you to solve?
Did it?
you know...
I once heard a wise woman say...

> FATHER is a name that one earns,
> you can't purchase it.

think about it.

Daniela
New Jersey
Age 15

One Sad Day

One sad day,
when I was very small,
my father went away,
not to come back at all.
I remember my mother's face,
stained with a tear.
I remember my face,
as she said, "Don't worry dear."
I couldn't bear the fact,
or even comprehend,
that he wasn't coming,
ever again.
Mom said not to worry,
that life would go on.
My whole world turned blurry,
as she sang me a song.
As she was singing,
I thought to myself,
that she would take care of me,
all by herself.
One sad day.

Brianna
Texas
Age 13

That Empty Spot

I wish that you could be right here,
To drive away all the fear.
Take the place of my step-father,
I don't think it would bother.

If you would come again,
Then my world would just begin.
Just take a look at me,
Nine years of sadness is what you'll see.

If you take a single look,
Half of my heart is what he took.
July 1st was the day,
It was the day he went away.

Brittany
Illinois
Age 11

To My Daddy

You said—
you would be there for us,
but you are not.

Why tell my mom—
you would be there,
when you knew you would not.

When I was younger—
I believed you would be there,
and not leave me,
but that was a lie.

I hope you know—
you hurt me,
but I know you don't care.

Becky
Colorado
Age 14

(Mother) Do You Ever Think of ME?

Sometimes I think about you
   Like where could you be?
Sometimes I ask myself
   Was it because of me?
Was it because of me you went away,
   Or did you have another plan?
I want to remember when I was your little girl
   And you would hold my hand.
Those times, they seem so long ago,
   Do you ever think of me?
Sometimes, I think I see you, then realize
   It's all in my mind.
What would it be like to see you
   Again, after all this time?
I don't know how I'd react,
   I don't know if I could speak.
Sometimes I think about you,
   Like where could you be?
Sometimes I sit and wonder,
   Do you ever think of me?

Stacy
Texas
Age 17

My Father

Memories now return since he left me,
Those memories are so vivid of the divorce when he moved away.
He was the best father to me.
Now he lives in Las Vegas so far away.

Those days before my father left were warm and golden.
We spent a lot of time together.
But now the days are cold and not so golden.
Now, I don't have my father.

He left me when I was five, so young.
I always think of him as if he's still here.
And now I'm not that young.
But the memories are still very near.

Jamie
Wyoming
Age 11

Alone

I remember a day when I was young
he said he had to go.
Mom said we would start over,
so we left the house empty and alone.

I'm still waiting for him to come home.
After years of waiting I guess he's not coming.
I hope one day I can understand why he left us alone.

Jeanna
Pennsylvania
Age 13

A Family Broken

From the moment I heard my dad was leaving
I wanted to cry and I started screaming.
Why is this happening to me I said
Why is my daddy going away.
My mom told me that everything is going to be alright
But how could I believe her when they always seemed to fight.
My eyes just started to fill up with tears
I thought, "What would I do without my daddy here."
He has been there for me through good times and bad
But now he has left and it makes me sad.
I learned that even though my parents are not together
They will both always love me forever and ever.

Shelly
Louisiana
Age 16

you are missing my life

Where Were You?

You were there for my birth.
You were there for my first words.
You were there for my first steps.
You were there for my birthday.

Then things changed.
You and mommy started fighting.
Then one day you left.

So where were you for my first day of school?
Where were you for my first basketball game?
Where were you when I got braces?
Where were you when I had friend problems?
Where were you when I had boy problems?

Where were you when things got tough?
Where were you when I felt abandoned and alone?
Where were you when I felt the world was too good for me?
Where were you when I needed you the most?

I guess what I really want to know is
Where were you?

Jessica
Iowa
Age 13

Why?

Why does he not want to see me?
    Always staying away, not watching.
    Always missing the moments
    I wish he could see,
    Always with his other family,
    What about me?
        I am his, too.
    I don't think he really cares anymore,
    Like he's become immune to feelings.
Why?

Cameron
Tennessee
Age 13

Daddy's Little Girl

I once was known as *Daddy's Little Girl*
He made sure everyone knew it too
He would make me feel like the only little girl he ever loved...
He was always there to heal my wounds both mentally and physically
He would also always take care of me when I was sick
He always had some kind of family cure for a slight fever (they were pretty
weird, but it always worked)
He was always there for me

I was no longer *Daddy's Little Girl*
He left me at a very young age
He left me for another woman and three other *DADDY'S LITTLE GIRLS*!
He would no longer be there to heal my wounds both mentally and physically
He would no longer take care of me when I was sick
He would no longer be there to try weird cures for a slight fever
He would no longer be there for me
He would no longer love me like he used to

Now I'm 14 and I long to be *Daddy's Little Girl*
But I no longer can
He made a choice that affected my life dramatically
He would probably say I was jealous
He doesn't realize I can't bear his loss
And I am jealous...

Rena
New Mexico
Age 14

My Father

Whenever I smell
pine cones
it is Washington in April 1984,
and I am running
gaily through my dad's backyard
playing with the little yellow duck
he had given me,
and being a kid at heart.

The sun shines beams
through the yellow strands
of my hair as my dad gently
holds me in his arms.

But this is not my story.
My story is my dad being absent
in the years of my life
forgetting
the daughter
he once had.

April
Nebraska
Age 18

Dear Dad

Even though I don't know you very well,
you can't blame me.
It was your fault, your loss.
You acted as if you loved me.
Then the day came
when you never picked me up.
That night my mom was there for me
when you should have been.
Later the letters came,
saying you just didn't have time.
I was so young,
I didn't know what life would be
without a dad.
Apparently you didn't care
about my feelings or needs.
Now I am older
I don't feel sorry anymore.
I have a good life
even without you in it.

Stephanie
Pennsylvania
Age 14

My "So-Called" Dad

When I was two,
My sister was two months.
A man we barely knew
Moved far, far away.

He forgot about us on our birthdays,
He forgot about us on Christmas,
He never called us to see how we were
'Till many, many years later.

Two years ago,
He moved again.
Hadn't seen us for two years,
And when he did, he just complained.

Now he's giving up his rights,
And I'm not the least bit sad.
For all I care, he could've done it years ago.
This man we called "Dad."

Ross
South Dakota
Age 13

Good Night

I sat on your lap as you cut the cake
Six candles still stood on top
I blew them out as fast as I could
'Cuz the wax had started to drop.
"The birthday girl gets the very first piece,"
You'd say with a wink, so I'd see.
You took a bite of my birthday cake,
So I yelled, "But the birthday girl's me!"

You gave me the cake and I smiled
At you 'cuz nobody else could see that
The frosting had gotten on your mustache.
Nobody had to tell me that
Your body was shaking when you said good-bye

And I felt a tear on my shirt.
I was only six, and I didn't realize
How much that it would hurt.
You couldn't remember my seventh or eighth,
Not a birthday card in sight.
You drove off and away
That's the last I saw you.
I just wanted to say, "Good night."

Emily
California
Age 12

Somewhere Out There

How long are you going to stay away?
You've already been gone a lifetime.
Can't you come and kiss me good night?
A lullaby?
What's the matter—
Are you scared?
I won't send you away.
I need you to be in the picture again.
What's ten years?
A family and a father are nothing to lose—
In comparison to what we'd have if you returned.
Maybe just one night.
I'll stay awake—
And we can talk about
High school sweethearts,
And a childhood spent in the sun.
Snow to sand—
Pine to palm—
Daddy to daughter—
Everything you've missed.

Heather
Pennsylvania
Age 16

The Father I Never Knew

You never called, you said you would.
You were supposed to do all the things a dad should.

We never went out and had lots of fun,
Or played baseball in the warm sun.

Mom said you were leaving for a while,
But that was when I was a little child.

Now I'm grown up no more games to play,
The teddy bears are put away.

For life is short, the years rush past,
A little boy grows up so fast.

I needed to know you loved and cared.
What happened to the love we both shared?

From now on we'll be like strangers.
No more can I hide all these angers.

Lauren
Ohio
Age 12

Where is My Dad?

He comes around like he cares,
but when I was young he was not there.
He has a new family and a wife to love dear,
when I was around he made me feel weird.
When I was alone crying in my bed,
was he there, no, it was mom instead.
When I look at my friends with their moms and dads,
I think if he didn't mess it up,
Oh what I could have!

Dana
Pennsylvania
Age 13

Regret

When I look back on my life for memories of you I find myself searching.

That of what I do find is meaningless.

They're not so much memories as they are vague images of someone I wish I knew.

I'm unable to find memories of you being there during my greatest achievements or being there during my worst let downs.

Even during all the times I've cried in happiness and in sadness, after I wiped away all the tears, I always found myself asking, "where are you?"

I've been asking this question my entire life.

However, as naive as it may be, I feel that maybe someday you'll become a part of my life.

Maybe someday I'll know you as a father and not a support check.

Of course there is one problem.

A lifetime only lasts so long.

Ardell
Pennsylvania
Age 14

Dear Daddy

Why?
Why did you go?
Don't you love me?
Mom says you do
but I'm not so sure.
You didn't even
call on my birthday,
don't you know when it is?

I'm in high school now,
did you know that?
I'm 14 did you know that?
I'm on the softball
team did you know that?

When I was little you
said you would always
be there for me, well
the truth is you're not

Rachel
Ohio
Age 14

i don't love you

Nine

I don't remember the exact day that it began.
Or the sweater I was wearing when my parents
"began their war against each other."
My sisters and I became the child hostages.
I was nine years old.

I remember my oldest sister,
coaxing me to wake up to the screaming fight of my parents in the kitchen.
She lovingly wrapped my Strawberry Shortcake blanket
around my shoulders as we ran barefoot through the snow
to take refuge with a neighbor.
I was nine years old.

My mother sat me down to tell me all the reasons to hate my dad.
And she arranged more mother-daughter days, to further preach her cause.
This is when I grew to hate my father— when I was nine years old.

But then I thought for myself and began to blame both my parents
for the hell that they've selfishly dragged their children through.
This is when I grew to hate my parents.
And this is when I grew to hate men. And this is when I grew to hate divorce.
And this is when I grew to hate love. And this is when I grew to hate.
When I was nine years old.

Jessica Dillon
New York
Age 17

Emptiness

Inside of me is a huge emptiness,
This emptiness is created by the family
I never had,
And memories I used to have and
Choose to forget about.

You are unable to know how I feel
You think it's just a stage
I feel it is a bit more than that
The emptiness is created by you

You were never there
And want to be now
I hate you
So why don't you let me go

Whitney
Ohio
Age 13

Life With My Father

On a spring day sitting in the grass with my family,
But no father
Mother loves my brother and I
I am sad that my father is gone.

He is not dead but still is not here,
Mother and Father are divorced what choice do we have,
Father is not that near,
I should miss him but I don't.

I live with my mom and older brother,
My dad lives in Laramie without us,
Mother loves me and tries to take care of both of us.
My brother and I don't really miss our dad.

Noah
Wyoming
Age 11

I Remember

I remember when you were there,
I remember that he wasn't.
Always in prison, always away
Never called, not a day.
I remember how you said, "Don't worry."
I remember how I always did.
I remember when he got out.
I remember the walk down the street.
I remember how he stepped on my feet.
I remember how he got married one day.
I remember how his life slipped away.
I remember him in prison again.
I remember him saying, "Never again."
I remember the divorce.
I remember all these things of course.
You may not think I know the truth,
He doesn't love me or you.
As our father left for the last time,
I thought one more chance is his last.
But then again I thought it through,
That was his last. I paid my dues.

Andrea
Alabama
Age 13

Daddy's Little Girl

How could you leave me standing all alone?
You made me, you raised me, and now you're gone.
And after that, you took away our home.
For your love, for your touch I do so long.

I loved you so much, oh why can't you see
I need you now more than ever before.
If only you had time to talk with me.
But yet it seems that you try to ignore.

Now you've two daughters but they're not your own.
And you have Mrs. Barbie Doll for a wife.
But, what about me you've left all alone,
It's me your girl to whom you've given life.

Up till now I have had to compensate,
But what shall I do with all of this hate?

Ashley
Arkansas
Age 17

The Life of a Fatherless Child

Imagine a life filled with hate and grief.
Imagine a life with pain beyond belief.
Imagine a shadow that overtakes the light.
Imagine a child that prefers the night.
Imagine a father that never sees his son.
Now imagine a child that never has fun.
You will discover nothing but a black hole,
If you ever stare into the windows of his soul.
You may think your life is pretty wild,
But it's nothing compared to the life of a fatherless child.

Matthew
New Jersey
Age 15

i miss you

Daddy

I love you, Daddy
All the wonderful things we did together
All the talks we had
The games we played
I didn't like the bad things that happened
The drinking that you did
All the fights we had
And the yelling you did
The wonderful things are gone
I miss you, Daddy.

Amy
Illinois
Age 13

Daddy

I sit on my bed
Wondering if I'll ever see him
I cry myself to sleep and think
Does my Daddy love me?
I wake up the next morning
and the next, and the next . . .
Hoping I'll hear his voice on the phone.
He never calls.

Amanda
Massachusetts
Age 12

I'm Sorry

I stole the picture of my dad off my sister's shelf.
I love the picture
My father looks so manly and grown-up.
He was so handsome.
He did not know that someday he would have two daughters
Who would love him very much
And wish we could see him more.
But when my parents got divorced
They did not know it would break our hearts
Or that their youngest daughter would steal something
Just to see him, even in a picture.

Stephanie
New York
Age 12

Good-Bye
Not

Someone is forgotten.
Someone special.
Dad is forgotten by many,
But not me.
I can still hear Mom and Dad.
The anger in their voices.
And I,
So young,
Seven.
Too young to lose a Dad.
Too young to understand
No more midnight talks,
No more goodnight kisses.
No more Dad.
GOOD-BYE Not.

Amy
New York
Age 10

Blind

A man thoughtlessly goes away leaving behind
A wife and kids. How can he be so blind?
Why can't he see all the pain in their eyes,
As he packs his bags and leaves without saying good-bye.

His son thought of him as the best Dad in the world,
His daughter thought she was her "Daddy's Girl."
Now all that's gone. He's taken it away
Without even telling them if he'd return someday.

He decided that his life was no longer "fun,"
And said to them all, "It's over, it's done."
Leaving his wife to do it all herself,
Taking care of the kids, as well as everything else.

The children begged and pleaded as he drove away,
To please come back, and please to stay.
He chose to ignore them, he didn't care,
Then he left in his car to a place, they didn't know where.

Didn't he love them at all? How could he just leave
A family full of despair and grief?
They pray that they'll be strong as life goes on,
Without that one man in their lives for whom they all long.

Britt
Ohio
Age 13

My Mom

When my mom moved away
We were all very sad
I wanted her to stay,
So I could be glad

She moved out west
Across the county and up
She said "SEATTLE'S THE BEST!"
Yet I feel like an empty cup

We went to see her
My sister and I
During Spring break
And then again in July

That July
I wanted to leave
But when it was time
It was hard to say bye-bye!

Carrie
Ohio
Age 10

Broken Hearts

You said you would come,
But you never did.
I waited forever,
But you didn't come.
Sis and I were sad,
I had to take care of her
Because she had no real mother
That lived with her.
Our step-mom is always angry,
She hurt Sis and me.
We couldn't do anything
Cause she is huge.
Sis and I called you
When our step-mom wasn't home.
We could never go anywhere,
Our step-mom didn't trust us.
Sis and I miss you so much,
But you never call,
Or write,
You don't even visit.
We miss you, Mom.

Adrienne
Michigan
Age 10

Dad

Dad from all the years that you and mom have shared since I was a baby
I have noticed how happy I was just to be with you.
Now that it is all gone I'm still wishing I could be with you.

Dad, if it weren't for you and mom I would not be here today.
Life was great to have both of you at my side when I needed you the most.

But now that you're divorced,
I guess mom is always here to take my side when I need her.
I wish you were here to have that same chance.

Dad, I loved to hold you and Mom in my arms at the same time
and without having you in my arms, I wouldn't know what a real dad was like
without having you around each day to see me grow up.

Nicole
New Mexico
Age 14

Turned Away

When I was a little girl,
I never thought life would be this way,
It was that one word divorce that drew us away,
There were many choices that needed to be made,
It seems those choices were to be made everyday,
There were little times of laughter, mostly lots of tears,
But many times of tearful fears,
I never knew how much was really cared,
Until the moments were missed that we shared,
It really hurt to be turned away,
By my own father in every way,
And even though we're far apart,
He will always be in my heart!

Julie
Ohio
Age 17

Does He Love Me?

I always wonder does he love me
He never comes to see me
He never calls
He never writes
Sometimes I sit and wonder when I'll see him again
What did I do to deserve this
He used to send me birthday cards
But all of a sudden he stopped
I don't know where he is
I want him to be here
I feel that a part of me is missing
When will that missing part come back to me
Does he know how hard it is for me
I want him to be there for me when I need him
Sometimes I feel mad and hurt
Why does he do this to me
All I want to know is does he love me?

Kasi
Oklahoma
Age 11

Daddy

Sometimes I wonder, do you ever think of me?
And if you hadn't left, how our lives would be.
Do you remember my first tooth, or when I began to talk?
Do you remember how I'd smile at you, or when I began to walk?

Do you remember teaching me to cook,
Or how to put a worm on a hook?
Do you remember watching football with me
Sitting as close to you as I could be?

Do you remember rocking me to sleep, in your favorite chair?
Do you remember all those times I thought you cared?
Do you remember all those wonderful times we shared?
Do you know that I wish you were still here?

Do you miss me as much as I miss you?
Would you have done things differently if you only knew
That sometimes I wonder, do you ever think of me?
And if you hadn't left how our lives would be.

Tory
Oklahoma
Age 11

i will always love you

Pedal after Pedal

As my dad made his way down the road in a car made of metal,
I rode after him on my bike by pushing pedal after pedal.

Why he left I will never know,
And I know I would miss him so,
No matter where he went or no matter how far,
I'd say "I love you dad no matter where you are."

I do remember one day when my parents got into a fight,
It was a few days ago on a dark, gloomy night,
They screamed and yelled at each other, well that's what I heard,
They stopped the quarrel after I heard this one word.

"Divorce," which made my parents go to court,
What's worse is that I had to go too,
I hope what occurred will never happen to you.

"Mother," they said to me while I was lying in a chair,
I went home that day in my Mother's car,
But that all happened when I was a tike,
When I was still learning how to ride a bike.

Now I'm thirteen and in eighth grade,
I'm not really sure what happened on that day,
Father, I know that you are very far,
But I still love you no matter where you are.

Terence
Connecticut
Age 13

149

Dad

You told me not to cry,
Everything's going to be O.K.
But that was before you packed
And turned to drive away.

You told me to be brave,
You told me to show no fear.
But that was then,
And now you're not here.

I never got over you
Not being with me,
You opened my eyes to things
I said I couldn't see.

You hugged me when I was right
And scolded me when I was wrong
You taught me how to catch, Dad,
As you yelled, "Go long! Go long!"

Seven years have gone by, now
And still we live apart
But I will love you always, Dad.
Always in my heart.

Shannon
Michigan
Age 17

Father

My father is a role model,
he has a kind heart,
he is always there for me.
If I am troubled or discouraged
he tries to help me in any way he can.
My father is someone I can go to
with any problem that I have and
not worry about what he might say.
Even though I live in a totally different state
he is always there for me.

Nicole
Tennessee
Age 12

A Letter to Dad

Dad where were you when I turned five
Why don't you carry me on your shoulders anymore
How come you don't take me out for fun
How come you talk down to me
I love you

Dad why did you and mom divorce
How come you get mad at me
How come you ask me questions I don't know
How come you don't make me feel loved
I love you

Dad what happened
How come you are colder than December winds
How come you put me through misery every other weekend
How come you don't listen
WHY?

Micah
Indiana
Age 12

Why Me?

Does my Dad love me?
If so, why did he leave me?
I need him now, you see.
But of course, he is too busy for me!

My Dad is thirty-four.
He had a girlfriend, or maybe more.
He is not too busy for them,
But me.
How could this be?

When day has gone by
And darkness is upon the sky,
I sit in a chair
And ask myself: Why
Do I have time to spare
For a man like my dad
Who makes me so mad
That I want to cry?

I love my dad so much, you see.
But why can't he?
Why Me, God, Why me?
Please help me, God. Please!

Jessica
New York
Age 13

Incomplete

I love my dad with all my heart,
Though it seems like God wants us kept apart.
He lives over two thousand miles away,
I want to see him; give me one more day.
I live with my mom, not my dad,
And sometimes it makes me so sad.
I love them both so much
Though I can't hug my dad often;
I can't give him my touch.
It seems so easy to choose, to everyone I know,
But it's not; it's not, I now know.
No one understands the things I go through,
It wouldn't be as easy, if it happened to you.
I know I'll be with him, one final day
When will the day come; will it come my way?
God keep us together, don't make us stay apart,
Hopefully one day he'll have my heart.

Stephani
Alabama
Age 12

Daddy is Gone

Whispers in my ear, shadows before my eyes,
Tears upon my cheek begin to crystallize.
I am young, I know, but I understand
What has just happened between this woman and this man.
Both I love so dear, want to keep them near,
But when all they do is fight
I can't stand to have them in my sight.

I see he must be leaving, and my heart is bent on grieving.
I know their union won't last,
But I don't want him to be left in the past.
To see him disappear would leave a hole in my heart;
This growing fear could tear me apart.

He promised, said he'd always be around.
Oh how I've wished that he was somewhere to be found.
To hear his voice, to see his face,
To know I always have a place, in his heart
Where I long to be, just as I have done
With the memory of the man
Whom I love, whom I adore, whom I wish I could see once more.
The man that made me happy;
The man that I called "Daddy."

Amanda
Virginia
Age 17

I Want To Be Your Daughter Again

I want to be your little girl.
I want to share things with you.
I want you to cuddle me in your arms,
And tell me things I never knew.

I want you to love me for who I am.
I want to know where you've been.
I don't want to hurt you, Daddy,
But I want to be your daughter again.

I want you to know that I love you,
But we've grown apart in the years.
I want this to work before it's too late.
I don't want to shed any more tears.

It's hard for me to say this.
I hardly know where to begin.
I don't want to hurt you Daddy,
But I want to be your daughter again.

Andrea
Wisconsin
Age 14

Memories of a Father from Long, Long Ago

I will always remember the time I fell and hurt my leg,
    He was always there, always around to make me laugh.
Only four years old, he left my house and packed his bags for good.
    We ran on the beach, splashing round the cool, salty sea.
So many memories that scar my mind,
    Pancakes on a Sunday morn, cuts and bruises from running free.
But as time went on I saw him less, he had moved away from me,
    To be alone, and to be himself without worries of a family.
I saw him for the last time when I was seven,
    And thoughts flow freely through my mind, though only in short clips.
All I know is that those five days were filled with love,
    Together again, just like we always should have been.
We walked the streets of California, hand in hand,
    Father and daughter, joined together by love.
Eight years ago we were one, hand in hand, father and daughter,
    Like nothing had ever changed.
Now all that remains of my dad is a tattered old picture,
    A few memories and a broken heart with an empty space.
But no matter how far or how long we're apart,
    I'll always remember my dad and I.

Amanda
Virginia
Age 15

My Parents

My mom is like the sun,
My dad is like the moon.
They are opposite, separate and different.

My mom is a female,
My dad is a male,
They are opposite genders.

My mom lives with me,
My dad doesn't live with me.
They are separate.

My mom likes the sunlight,
My dad likes the moonlight.
They are different, but...

They both love me the same!

Olympia
Minnesota
Age 9

Broken Families

Although I live with my mom,
I really love my dad.
My dad is really great.

My mom may not agree with me,
That really makes me sad.

I wish I could be with my dad,
That dream would not come true.
Until then I will still love my dad,
But I'll love my mother too,
Even though I may not agree with her.

I have a split life—it splits right in two.
Half my mother,
Half my father, too.

I love them both equally,
I don't play favorites like parents do.
I hope this has touched you,
Like it has touched me too!

Sean
Maryland
Age 9

Daddy

You left me.

You left me alone.

You left me, a small child to face a big world.

You left me and thought I didn't understand.

You left me, but I knew, never asking "Where's Daddy?" because I knew.

You left me, calling every Sunday, "How's school? How are your friends? How's your Life without a Daddy?"

You left me, and for as long as I can remember I had to take a plane just to see you.

You left me, and I saw my friends with their Daddys and me without mine.

You left me to my new "father," cold and undaddy-like.

You left me, missing my accomplishments; sports, report cards, musicals.

You left me, Daddy, I'll never forgive you.

You left me, Daddy, somehow I still love you.

Jessica
Pennsylvania
Age 16

i want my family back

Mother and Father Not Together

Mother and Father not together,
sometimes I feel sad and I cry.
I think about Daddy a whole lot.
I go to my room and sit down
and dream about them talking,
about moving into the same house together.
I say in my brain, "Please, Lord, let them
move in the same house, please Lord,
let them move in the same house."

Brandon
North Carolina
Age 11

Come Back to Us

We were all together once before
What happened? I don't know.
I wish that you could understand the way I feel.
I know you don't approve of what I do,
But you should be there by my side.
The stuff that's going on
Is making me lose the love inside.
Why can't we just be a family again?
We've been through hard times
But nothing should stop the feelings we share.
You know the love always needs to be there.
The feelings now are as low as the ground,
And most of the time I frown.
Why can't we be the same
As we used to be?

Victoria
North Carolina
Age 14

Splitting up

My dad has gone away
I want him to come back to me
And forever stay

I love my dad
And I know that he loves me
I want them back together

But I guess it's not my choice!

Jessica
Illinois
Age 12

Dad

Dad moved out, and away from me
Dad didn't stay, he moved away from us
Us is me, my brother, and Mom.

I wish he'd come back, back to me
I hope he'll come back, back to us.

Three of us, we do just fine,
Four of us that's the pleasure of mine.

In my dreams he is with me
In my fantasy he is here
In the future I'd like him to be near.

Stephen
Connecticut
Age 12

Mom and Dad...

Mom...
Dad...
I wish it would all stop
My mind is tired, my heart can't quit crying.
This fighting and this lonely feeling inside,
I don't want to deal with it any more.
It is making me crazy.
I just want my family back,
All together as one again.
I wish it all wasn't so hard.
I know you could love and be happy once more.
Just try.
We can all try.
I just want this all to go away.
This hollow feeling in my heart
Wants to be filled once again.

Alicia
Minnesota
Age 17

Divorce

I used to be happy
How I miss those days
Who knew my life would change
One word was all it took
One word and my life turned to dirt

Divorce is the word
I thought I'd never have to hear
Divorce is the word
Now here comes my worst fear

As we drive away, my dad standing at the porch
I turn around to get one last look
One look and my heart began to break
One look and my life turned gray

Now 3 years later
I still feel the pain
Now 3 years later
I still remember that day

I wish I had my family back
Or at least a place to call home
I wish I had a mom and dad
Who would at least talk on the phone

Alicia
California
Age 15

Dear Daddy

I think it was the special way you said it:
It made it so much easier to take.
You made it sound like you hated it,
But knew it was something you had to do.
That day you came to me and said,
"I'm leaving you."

It broke my heart and Mama's, too.
To know we can't be seeing you.
Brother's taking care and Mom's doing fine.
Regretfully I'll never forget the day you said,
"I'm leaving you."

You continued to say
How it "Must be" this way...
It just never seemed that way to me.

I've, in a way, understood
How you've been confused, misunderstood, and wrong.
It will be fine if you pray,
Then through God, may you repent.
Perhaps with a new heart you will,
Come back and be happier than ever.

Because we forgive you.

Rachel
Texas
Age 13

171

My Father

My father,
he named me.
We played together,
we slept together.
We cuddled together,
and ate together.
Then he left.

My father,
he taught me.
He taught me how to read,
he taught me how to play.
He taught me how to laugh,
he taught me how to cry.
Then he left.

My father,
he moved.
He hasn't called me,
he hasn't talked to me.
He hasn't cared for me,
he hasn't played with me.
Please move back.

David
Louisiana
Age 14

My Mom and Dad

My dad is a mechanic.

He works on cars and he is never around. Because my mom and dad got a divorce.

My mom works on air conditioners for cars. My mom works in Everman and my dad works in Irving.

I wish they were friends. But they do not have to be married. And I wish they would be together again.

So I can be happy.

My mom and dad are very special to me. And this is coming from my heart. I wish they were married again instead of apart. I love my mom and dad a lot. And I wish I could see my dad more often. So I could spend time with him. Like going bike riding on bike trails. Where I could show him I can go up a hill.

Ryan
Texas
Age 9

Back Together?

When my parents got together,
they thought they would be like that forever.
But when I was four,
they said they did not love each other any more.
Now it has been 9 years,
but I still have tears.
Will they ever get back together,
that is a question that will float around forever.

Shannon
North Carolina
Age 13

A Child's Life

A child's life may be fine in the beginning, middle and end,
But some children's lives may not be.
Some children's parents may be separated,
And their hearts are sore and their life is in pain.

When you grow up,
You never forget
The day your parents separated.
Your heart is still sore
With the pain.
I never thought that would happen,
My life is off course.

Your mind will never forget that day,
When you left your old house and moved away.
I always hope they will get back together,
But I know in my heart that it won't happen.

Stephanie
Michigan
Age 9

my two homes

Two Homes

I have two homes
each on the other side of town
my mom in one
my dad in the other
when I leave one house
to go to the other
a pain strikes
a pain of sorrow
but my happiness
is not left behind
I have two homes
one not better than the other

Darrel
Colorado
Age 10

Dear Dad

I feel abandoned
Is it me
Something I did
Something I said
You left

Talking once a week
through a thin wire
Cramming a week of my life in
fifteen minutes of time
isn't enough

Those two weeks a year I see you
are heaven
laughing, joking

Nothing can possibly go wrong
then the days are over
Time to let go

Then trying to be a man
not cry
not show emotion
Just get on the plane and go.

You love me, right?

Adam
Minnesota
Age 15

The Divorce

My mom and dad
Are not together
Because they don't
Care for each other
One goes this way
One goes that way
Which way to choose?
They both love me
They both care for me
Each has a grandma
Each has a grandpa
Which to decide?
But the court makes me go
To the one I know
That will always love me,
Will extend my education,
Will also buy me clothes
And all the other
One gets me is 4 days a
Month!!!!!!

Doug
Ohio
Age 11

daddy

my daddy left home when i was six
i saw him every other weekend for a while
he had a new wife and a new house and two new daughters
but he said i was still his daughter too

daddy had a dog
i was never allowed to have a dog when daddy lived with us
daddy started to wear flip-flops and go camping
he never did that before

daddy picked me up on Saturday morning
he dropped me back off Sunday night
i felt like i was spending the night at a friend's house
i was afraid to get a drink of kool-aid like i did at home

i would kiss daddy good-bye and go inside
i'd unload my overnight bag on the couch and go kiss mommy hello
i always forgot about daddy as soon as i walked through that door
i think he forgot about me too.

Chanda
Ohio
Age 16

The Day That Never Came

Standing on the edge of the curb
practicing my tight-rope walking
careful not to fall and ruin my new outfit
waiting and waiting...

I touch my perfectly combed hair,
made my mommy fix it twice,
make faces at the wind, daring it to mess my pigtails
waiting and waiting...

I look at my fidgeting brothers who decide to play basketball
thinking how silly they are, they'll get dirty
But I won't, so I stare down the street
waiting and waiting...

Zoom, Zoom the cars go by,
I watch each, hoping it will be the one
Time drags on and I try to stay still, standing there
waiting and waiting...

The night comes.
I am still waiting when
my mother calls me in,
my father had forgotten me, again.

Melissa
Texas
Age 17

When I'm With My Dad

When I'm with my dad that lives far away,
I feel happy,
I feel gay,
Sometimes I feel bad, depressed, or sad,
Because my heart gives a thump
Or a bump,
Only 'cause our homes are not the same.

Joshua
Washington
Age 9

3 Years Ago

My Mom and Dad got divorced
three years ago.
I hate it.

When my Mom comes to pick
me up they always fight.
I hate it.

When I get to my Mom's house
she treats me like trash.
I hate it.

When I get back to my Dad's
house he always yells at me.
I hate it.

My Mom and Dad got
divorced.
I hate it.

Laurie
Oregon
Age 9

My Mom Lives Here, My Dad Lives There

My Mom lives here,
My Dad lives there.
My brother and I live everywhere.

My brother and I bring clothes there,
We leave clothes here.
We bring and leave toys everywhere.
We love them both...
                    even though...
My Mom lives here and
My Dad lives there.

Stephanie
New York
Age 9

Two Homes

I have two homes
Two different places
One at my Mom's
One at my Dad's
On weekends I'm here
On weekends I'm there
So really I'm everywhere
One is in the city
One is in the country
One place I have a doggy
And another place I have a kitty
I have a room here
I have a room there
I have friends here
I have friends there
My friends are everywhere!
Sometimes it's great
Just fine
I wouldn't change a thing
Not in this lifetime
Because both families
Are all mine!

Samantha
Maryland
Age 9

I'll Never Know

I'll never know what could've been
If you and dad were still together
You got divorced when I was only two
I never knew what happened
I know now that I'm older
If you had stayed together, it would not have been pleasant
But it's hard for me you know
I remember when I was little
I would always miss my daddy
But when I got to dad's
I would always cry for mommy
Parts of life have been hard for me
Having to live in two separate worlds
Never really having the best of both parents at the same time
But I've gotten used to it
Getting dependent on either parent for different things
Yet there have been times
Where I wanted both or the other
And my wish was not granted
I'll never know what could've been
And I'm sure I never will

Emily
Illinois
Age 13

My Two Homes

Most people have one home,
but I have two.
One of my homes is with my
Mom.
My other home is with my
Dad.
I know they love me.
That's why I like having
My two homes.

Amanda
Ohio
Age 12

My Two Homes

My two homes are with my mom and dad.
It's more than one, it makes me sad.

It's fun when Christmas comes and birthdays, too!
Because there's lots of presents for you know who.

I'm never sure at which home I'll be.
But, I do know they both love me.

Jenna
Florida
Age 9

my evolving
family tree

My Big Family

I have a big family,
Four sisters, eight brothers,
Step mom and a step dad
My mom and my dad
We are quite a family.
My dad and step mom,
And we six boys
Live in a two-story house
With an old out-house.
We visit our mom and
Our three sisters,
On weekends, twice a month.
We play many games.
We go shopping a lot.
The time together
Seems all too short.

Doug
Nebraska
Age 13

My Father

I don't know my father.
What am I to do, when I finally do?
Will he love me?
Will he reject me?
Will he remember me?
What am I to do?
Does he think of me?
I sure do think of him!
Who is he?
What is he like?
Is he even alive?
Those are questions I ask myself every day,
So, where are you???

Now, I noticed that my father has been here all along.
He has been here to see me grow big and strong.
That is the only father I need.
He is *my* daddy indeed.

Nadja
West Virginia
Age 13

When the Divorce Happens

Right after the divorce,
I poured out in tears.
I thought I was the one who caused it.
But now I don't care,
Because he never spent time with me.
When I wanted to go somewhere,
He never came.
But now I have a step-dad,
Who buys me things I want.
We play board games together,
And do father and son things.
But best of all,
He cares.

Dan
Pennsylvania
Age 13

Step-dad

A dad who you can't trust,
Is a dad like mine.
Who is never there for you.
When you need a shoulder
To cry on, or love.
That is why I have a step-dad.
Who loves me more than life.
Who I can trust,
And love.
Who has a shoulder for me
To cry on.
That's why I love
My stepdad.

Amanda
Connecticut
Age 12

Dads

There are two guys I know
who sort of know each other
one was there to see you born
the other lives with your mother

Two different lives
that help to make your one
one is your guiding star
the other is your sun

One helped give you a name
the other is around to say it
one gave you a seed of talent
but they both give you an aim

One helped give you emotions
the other is learning to calm your fears
one saw your first home run
while the other one cheered

One had to leave
it was all that he could do
the other prayed for a family
and God sent him straight to you

Crystal
Ohio
Age 16

Stepfather

I met a special someone of my mom's one day
who soon became my step dad.
I've noticed I'm happier now that
I have him.
What I mean is that one day he's
gonna grab your love.

He always makes me smile,
even though I'm sad inside.
That's what stepfathers are for,
to give you love and happiness.
I pray, he will leave my mother–never
I love you Stepfather!

Bertha
Texas
Age 13

Suddenly You Turn Around and . . .

One day you see a six-year old boy.
He's in the living room in his house.
His mom comes in and tells him
That she and his dad are getting divorced.
The boy starts crying and getting mad.
The father gets his stuff and gets in his white truck
And leaves, never to come back.
The father moves in with his mistress.
The boy goes to see his father.
The boy is very troubled.
The mom sends the boy to counseling.
The boy stays up at night crying.
The mom has new boyfriends.
The boy hates the new men in his mom's life.
The boy's dad all of a sudden disappears out of his life.
The boy's mom finds a man to take the dad's place.
The boy is happy once again.
Or is he?

Kevin
Louisiana
Age 14

New Mother

She comes to take my mother's place.
but, I like the way she talks with me.

She makes me feel warm inside,
and she always seems to care.

Often times we both get mad
and have to settle things with Dad.

At least we both care about each other.
I am sort of getting used to my new mother.

Alicia
California
Age 13

Step Moms

When someone says step mom
It makes them sound so bad
They're not here to punish you
Or make you feel sad

Even though it might seem
They make your life worse
Don't start to hate them
Try being friends first

Once you're friends
Maybe you'll see
That it isn't as bad
As you thought it would be

Trust me, I would know
I have a step mom too
And at first I didn't like her
But now I really do

She's so important to me
In my life today
I'll love her always and forever
In every single way

Tracy
Illinois
Age 14

Step-mother

She came to us five years ago
My dad married her within a year
We all moved to a big, white house
Within the fine town of Windsor.

The house always has to be spotless
If it isn't, she will punish you
Most of the time she is nice
But sometimes she can be very irritable.
Solely, I love her all the same.

I think my true mom is sometimes jealous
She is jealous because my stepmom gets
To see me all the time.
They both dislike each other
Though my mom not as much
But I hope someday they will be friends.
Solely until then, I'll love them
But (NOT) as much.

Danny
California
Age 10

Divorce

When your parents get separated,
It's not easy you see.
They fight a lot,
And most of the fighting is over me.
I feel like it's all my fault,
But it really isn't.
Sometimes I cry myself to sleep at night,
Wondering why they did it.
Then someone new enters my life,
I don't know who they are.
I find out later, this will be my new mom.
I don't understand at first,
For I already have a mom.
Then I understand this is my second mom.
She's there for me when I need her,
Even though she has her bad days.
My mom has no one by her side,
We only see her every other weekend,
No one ever calls her,
And I always wonder why.

Jessica
Pennsylvania
Age 13

My Dad

I wish I could see my dad,
But I can't because his wife won't let him.
My mom said he could but he won't.
The only time I really see him is on holidays,
And he has to sneak over
So his wife won't know where he is.
He always gives stuff to me and my sister,
Stuff for Christmas, birthdays, and all other holidays.
He tells me to call him at work,
I do sometimes but not always.

Nikki
Michigan
Age 11

It'll Happen Again

Each month my mom and step-dad start to fight.
My mom has talked about it on the phone.
I heard her mention the horrible sight.
"He has a bad temper and a dreadful tone."

When the time comes, he usually leaves.
To tell you the truth, this makes me glad.
Because at this time the house is at ease.
Though you can see, my mom is oh so sad!

I know in life, there will be hardships to face.
And with all my troubles I'd say I'm doing well.
No longer do I feel he's taking too much space.
On what happened in the past, I will not dwell.

I think they will be back together in a while.
Until then, I'll just cooperate and smile!

Bethany
Louisiana
Age 11

Intertwine

It hangs in my room
on the wall behind my bed
reminding me of memories long ago.
It shows the way my family used to be
before the numbers began to descend.
This one tells of misery and betrayal
but shows some of my closest friends.

Beside it, is a new family,
I'm also in this one.
No longer my sister's face appears
but four new ones.
My mother's face
is only reflected by my own.
And taking her place is someone new
who has taken her place in our home,
but not in our hearts.
My dad is still hovering
over this family as he is in the other.
The "Great Peacemaker."

As I look at them, I can see my life
as being two trying to intertwine as one.

Cari
South Carolina
Age 17

i'm still standing

Dominoes

My world is like dominoes,
Everything is falling down.
But I stand tall,
High on sturdy ground.
My dad is leaving,
Me and my mom are moving.
This is not very pleasing.
But I still push on.

My heart is crushed, just as their marriage was,
But I still stand tall—
On sturdy ground.
I still cry, but I am very brave.
Why did this happen?
Why today?
I am still standing tall—
right in the center.

My world will never be the same,
But, I'm still standing and
My dominoes are still falling.
Maybe one day
My dominoes will stand with me too.

Katie
Texas
Age 9

Lives Do Change

Divorce can be pretty tough on a nine-year-old kid,
That's how old I was when it happened to me,
At first I thought it was my sister's fault,
Then I thought it was my brother's fault,
Then, sadly, I thought it was my fault,
It is hard when a kid has to go through that,
I got used to my dad not being there,
Although it was painful and stressful at first,
It got better,
Kids go through a lot more than people think,
We went through hard times,
Then it got a whole lot better,
It's not as bad as it seems.
Now we are "very" happy,
And now I have a wonderful step-dad named Tom!

Cristine
Ohio
Age 13

Everything is Okay After All

Three feet tall and only forty pounds, I was the man of the house.
I had so many emotions for a little guy only six years old.
I felt sad, angry, lonely and scared.
You see, my mom and dad were getting a divorce.
I couldn't even say the word refrigerator clearly,
And I had never heard the word divorce before.
All I knew is that my dad was not going to live with us any more.
I felt like I had the weight of the world on my shoulders.
My mom told me things would be okay, but I was really scared.
I will never forget how I felt back then.
But you know what, mom was right.
Now several years later I have a new stepdad, and my dad just got married.
The best part was, I was the best man in the wedding.
And you know what, everything is okay after all.

Peter
Pennsylvania
Age 12

Divorce...

the word pierces me like an arrow
the memories of the screaming
and arguing and slamming doors
and pulling away in a car
leaving daddy behind
why i asked myself
what i did to deserve this
don't they love me anymore
why would they do this to me
maybe if i prayed hard enough
or if i was really good
mommy and daddy would get back together
now ten years later
things have changed some
but mommy and daddy
still live in separate houses with separate families
but the fights have ended
and mommy and daddy are happy
and they still love me just as much

Meghan
New York
Age 16

Ups and Downs

When my parents got divorced,
I thought my world would end.
I thought there would be hate
Between my parents.
My thoughts were wrong.
My world didn't end,
It just got bigger.
There was no hate between my parents,
Just friendship.

I have double the chores,
But double the money.
I have twice the fights,
But twice the fun.
I have two rooms to keep clean,
But two rooms full of stuff.
I have two times the pets,
But two times the clean up.

There are ups and downs,
Of having divorced parents.
But no matter if they're together or not,
I know they will always love me.

Rachel
Oregon
Age 12

the split

the split took place when I was young
not knowing any better I thought it was my fault
memories lasting, details vivid
angry voices creeping through the wall
hours on end that was all that was heard
then nothing...silence
waiting for an explanation, a lie to tell me why
eventually the arguments become constant
until one day it was over in an instant
mother kept me at her side leaving father to fend for himself
years have passed, wounds have healed, scars remain
father still loves as does mother
they communicate for no other reason than their children
for that reason I love them both

John
Pennsylvania
Age 15

Hurt

Laying in my bed
Crying myself to sleep
My brother in my head
Hurt, I feel so deep

Wondering what he's doing
If he's even thinking of me
In my dreams he's always sitting
And his face I never see

If only we were together
Like we used to be
Our mother and our father
We thought were married happily
Hurt, I feel so deep

Everything happened so fast
Like a roller coaster ride
Where the rush doesn't last
I wanted badly a place to hide

I have gone through it all
And one thing I have learned
Is even when so deep you fall
To a high level you can always return

Andrea
Oregon
Age 14

Painful Divorce

All the love and happiness that came from the heart,
Soon went away as they drifted apart,
All the hatred that was growing inside,
Came out all at once like someone had just lied,
I hate you, I hate this, I don't love you anymore,
One of them said as they ran out the door,
The papers were signed and the trial was done,
As they left behind a beautiful daughter and a wonderful son,
The marriage was over with a sudden drop,
But the lives of the now separate families will never stop,
All the pain and anger was for the best,
At least now, everything is at rest.

Heather
Washington
Age 14

A Cry For Help

Is it something I said? Could I have helped?
Is it my fault? Why is this happening to me?
I don't know where to turn; I don't know what to do.
My head is spinning and I can't understand.

My life is fine just the way it is. I don't want to change it.
My parents tell me that the divorce isn't my fault but theirs.
I can't accept this. Surely I could have helped.
Such a rush of emotions and nobody here to help.
Nobody to understand, nobody to listen.

I just want someone to listen to me as I clear my mind,
To be there as a shoulder to cry on.
I don't deserve this, I wish it wasn't me,
I wish this would happen to anyone but me.

This is how I used to think, now I am different.
I am not happy for the divorce, only its effects on me.
It ripped my heart in two and humbled me beyond belief.
I have gained new wisdom and insight to the minds of people.

I now understand how terrible and amazing it is at the same time.
Terrible because your whole world is torn apart.
Amazing because it makes you even stronger than before.
My only wish is that everyone could understand the hurt and pain.

David
Kentucky
Age 14

Live On

When I was young, not older than six
My mommy and daddy just did not mix

They used to fight they used to yell
But I loved them both just as well

My brother and I used to cry
At that point I was very shy

I hate divorces they are really tough
More rough than all other stuff

Now I'm eleven and in grade seven
And I wish I could have a slice of heaven

I have one step-mother and one step-brother
I can't wish for any other

I wish there would be more pros than cons
I guess I have to keep living on

Mark
New York
Age 12

My Parents Divorced

When my parents got divorced,
I felt my world had ended.

I always thought it was my fault,
My crying never ended.

I always use to think,
Why did God do this to me?

My parents said, "This is the best thing,
For both of us and also you."

It has been four years now,
Since my parents got divorced.

I've gotten on with my life,
But it took a lot of force.

Justine
New York
Age 13

It Will Get Better

Divorce is sad
It makes you mad
Too bad you can't change it
It starts
Never stops
Divorce hurts people
You and me
It feels like you were stung by a million bees
Someone leaves
So suddenly
It's like a changing tree
After time the hurt goes away
You learn to smile
And even play
So when you feel
Like your world is crashing down
Look up and put your feet back on the ground
It will get better
It always does

Alex
New York
Age 13

lessons i've
learned

Why Couldn't You Care?

You were there at the start
So wanting to care
With love in your heart
You said, "I'll be there!"

You thought and you wondered
Is he really mine?
Then you decided
For this little one I have no time.

Alone Mom raised me
Always wanting you there
She would call and she'd write
But you'd never care

Mom tried to fill in
With stuff all Dads do
Let's face it Dad
She isn't quite you

I love you Dad
I'll say this too
But I'll never grow up
To be just like you!

Jason
California
Age 13

The Nightmare

Divorce is a thing that happens with sadness,
Not everyone cooperates.
Then comes the time of passing from house to house,
But sometimes it does not happen with gladness.

Next, comes the time when marriage happens again,
And then adapting to your new stepparents.
Sometimes stepparents can be hard to deal with,
But parents are always there so you can depend.

Then my father might not pay child support,
And when he doesn't my mom gets frustrated.
I have fear that my parents will get lawyers,
They will sue each other and end up in court.

Tears flow down my face. I don't know what to do.
Then I go to bed and think of who I am.
Then I end up with an answer like this one:
Very complicated, but special too!

So please, I beg you desperately!
When your parents are divorced just hang in there.
And if they aren't you should be very glad,
Because your family will act more happily.

And also – to the married couples out there,
Work hard, give all you can to stay together.
And if you have any children, think of them,
Don't let them go through what I have (the nightmare!)

Keilani
California
Age 11

My Parents are Divorced

My parents are divorced
and it makes me sad.

Because I only see one at a time,
that doesn't make me glad.

I wish, I wish that my parents would kiss,
but that probably won't exist.

There are some things that are good
about my parents being divorced.

That I get twice the presents
and it teaches me not to get divorced.

Aaron
Rhode Island
Age 11

Dear Dad

Dear Dad,

    I am sorry
    For all the times I didn't see you
    At my soccer games,
    Your face beaming with pride,
    And I was whisked away by Mom,
    Not allowed to speak to you.
    I'm sorry for all of our visits
    Cut too short by Mom's punctuality.
    Arrival no earlier than 6 p.m.,
    Departure no later than 8 p.m.,
    And no extra time together.
    I'm sorry for every time you cried
    When I didn't want to be with you.
    But you never told me
    What I was doing to you.
    I'm sorry for all of the ways I hurt you.
    I didn't know any better.
    Only now do I realize your pain.
    Oh Daddy, I am sorry.

Jenna
Minnesota
Age 15

Five Years Ago

I walked inside one day
My dad told me
They were getting a divorce
I walked back outside

I was angry
I was sad
There were a bunch of mixed emotions
Something bad was happening in my life

It was for the best
Now they don't argue
Now they sit down and talk
I'm happier, a little bit

It's still a little sad
My parents aren't together
I'm going to wait a little longer
To find somebody right
I don't want my kids to go through this.

Josh
Indiana
Age 16

Empty Days

All those weeks gone by,
With mom getting up early,
Dad is nowhere,
That position is blank,
I never got the love I deserved.

I'd wake up every morning,
Confused and depressed.
How could you walk out on me?
Leaving such a big empty space,
A big hole in my heart.

I'd like to thank you now.
I know it had nothing to do with me,
But by the hell you put me through,
I became the person I am today.

Thanks.

Ashlee
Kansas
Age 17